Lusty

Tim Jenkins

This book is the work of over 38 years of experience of Tim Jenkins's life from the age of 11.

Scripture taken from the New American Standard Bible, © 1960,1962,1963,1968,1971,1972,1973,1975,1977 by the Lockman foundation. Used by permission."

All other scriptures have been taken from the King James Version (KJV) of the Bible.

Acknowledgements

As always, to God be the glory, the honor and the praise! For it's only because of God's mercy and grace that I'm able to pour out my heart to those who are willing to listen in the name of His dear Son, Jesus Christ.

I want to thank my beautiful wife for all of the love and support she's poured into my life. I love You Honey! I also love our 4 Children and 2 Grandchildren, thanks for being great Kids!

I want to thank the Body of Christ at Freedom Crossing for your dedication and support that you've given me as your Pastor and Brother in Christ Jesus. I love You all!

I want to thank my Uncle David and Aunt Debra Jenkins for the encouragement to write this book. God Bless You both and I love you!

Table of Contents

Foreword

*1 John 2:16 & 17 For all that is in the world, the **lust of the flesh**, and the **lust of the eyes**, and the **pride of life**, is not of the Father, but is of the world. and the world passes away, and the lust thereof: but he that doeth the will of God abides forever. (KJV)*

James 4:6 But He gives a greater grace. Therefore, it says, 'God is opposed to the proud, but gives grace to the humble. (NASB)

Proverbs 11:2 When pride comes, then comes dishonor, but with the humble is wisdom. (NASB)

Psalm 34:17 The righteous cry, and the LORD heareth, and delivereth them out of all their troubles. (KJV)

The Deliverance & Healing Ministry is one of the great blessings given to us by our Savior Jesus Christ right before he ascended into Heaven through the Great Commission.

*St. Mark 16: 17 – 18 And these signs shall follow them that believe; **In my name shall they cast out devils**; they shall speak with new tongues; They shall take up serpents; and if they drink any deadly thing, it shall not hurt them; **they shall lay hands on the sick, and they shall recover**. (KJV)*

*Ephesians 6:12 For our struggle **is not against flesh and blood,** but against the rulers, against the powers, against the world forces of this darkness, against the spiritual forces of wickedness in the heavenly places. (NASB)*

When I first heard the call to begin Deliverance Training Classes at our Church, I had no idea the Holy Spirit would have led us into such a wonderful but difficult part of the ministry.

Wonderful because of the people who were getting set free of demons but difficult because of so many who rejected it.

As time has gone on, the difficult part of being rejected has subsided but when you embark on a journey looking to bind and loose with force every demon that is tormenting the person the word difficult is an understatement.

However, I wouldn't change a thing because once you start witnessing the demons come out of people **St. Mark 16:17** comes alive in you. Once all of the demons have been evicted, you'll know it by the glow and huge smile that comes onto a person's face.

To see a depressed mentally ill person get set free without medication will change your life. After you see it and experience it, you'll understand why the 70 disciples came back to Jesus excited and the first thing that they said was this,

St. Luke 10:17 And the seventy returned again with joy, saying, Lord, even the devils are subject unto us through thy name. (KJV)

It doesn't matter what negative things the religious crowd says about deliverance, what matters is that Jesus gave us the commands to carry out the Great Commission. Who do you follow? The Deacon board or Jesus Christ?

Some in your religious circles may never allow you the opportunity to address your lust problem but don't give up God always sends help!

If you're a teacher or Pastor and you're struggling with sexual sin there's hope. These lust spirits are particular interested in destroying you because you're a Leader in the church. If these lust spirits succeed, they have a good chance of leading many to hell because of your downfall. Right now, you're a ticking timebomb and if not defused you will go off and the damage that you will cause will be devastating.

It's time to stop ignoring deliverance and get mad at Satan. Deliverance is not an option; you must face your demons today and put a stop to their harassment and torments in Jesus Name.

Introduction

I accepted Jesus Christ into my life at the age 10 but at the age of 11 I was faced with a giant. A giant presumably so big I just accepted it was something I would have to deal with for the rest of my life.

Even as a young boy growing into teenage life, I realized these same giants dominated many of my friends and even family. When these giants approached with opportunities my friends and some of my male family members would encourage me to participate in the offers.

Even though, what the giants offered felt good to my body, inside I was ridiculed with guilt and shame.

As a Pastor's son, no one would talk about such things. Even in the church services these giants were mentioned but were only dealt with in a short confession at the altar.

Confession is good but, what we need is deliverance and healing.

Jesus was my Savior but, these giants came and went as they pleased and the older I got — the harder it got.
It seemed hopeless but the more I read my Bible the more I realized that these giants could be defeated.
Knowing now that these giants could be defeated, I set out on a journey of no return.

Many times, I would ask God, "Just defeat them now for me, You're God, You can do all things." But God doesn't work that way. He's willing to give all of the help needed but he needs us to act as well. Training time! The Holy Spirit and our great teacher reveal to us, men in the Bible who had to go through training before facing their giants.

King David defended his father's sheep as a young boy and even risked his life for the sheep and killed a lion and a bear. Defending something else besides himself prepared him for the day that he would face a giant more destructive than a lion or a bear, GOLIATH! **(1 Samuel 17)**.

This book comes from my heart to the ones in secret who are crying out for help. Hope and deliverance come through Jesus Christ and the power of the Holy Spirit. I pray this book will help you fall in love with God's word and will help you overcome the giant of Lust and all of Satan's other evil spirits that he uses against you.

These giants you face can be defeated and you can be delivered from the hands of the tormentors. What you'll realize by the end of this book is that these giants aren't really giants at all, but fearful evil spirits who know that their days are numbered.

Chapter 1

My Testimony

At the age of 11, I saw my first pornographic magazine. I felt so guilty but my body responded in a way I had never felt before. My young body produced the natural chemicals that excited me and caused me to become aroused. I had no idea what was going on but it felt good.

My neighbor stole on older brother's porn magazine and he hid it in the woods between our houses. The longing to go look more and more was overwhelming. Then one day I went to look at it, and it was gone. But the damage had already been done. No orgasm but I was aroused and had felt the chemical releases of arousal. I longed for more.

Not long, after this incident, cable tv came into my house and it was filled with rated "R" movies and music videos which I sneaked and watched when I could. Nudity, cursing and sex were introduced to me through a television screen and thus began a long road of disappointments.

At age 12, I was told about by a schoolmate about masturbation and once I learned how to do it, then came the fantasy world. This fantasy world grew by watching more television and listening to more secular music. My whole world was turned into selfishness, lust, and pride.

Before the age of 11, I wasn't a perfect kid but I always had respected women. After I saw what women portrayed on the movie screen, I began to see them as objects and not as God's creation. Lust had taken its grip on me but I thought that lust's grip on me had just started at age 11. What I realized later on in my life was that lust was an evil spirit which in turn was connected to all kinds of other evil spirits which were passed down through the family tree.

What I was experiencing from age 11 were generational demons that had been in our family tree possibly for centuries. My ancestors had a history of adultery and fornication and this history had not been dealt with—all the way down to me.

I quit church at age 17 and stayed out into the world for three years fulfilling my lustful desires. It seemed this was the life—I did what I wanted when I wanted, I had sex with whoever would sleep with me, and I drank and ate whatever and whenever I wanted. It was a selfish, miserable life.

At almost the age of 21, I had a truck accident. While the accident was in progress, my truck rolled over — like I was in slow motion and my life was flashing before my eyes. Great fear fell on me at that moment and I thought I was on my way to hell.

After being released from the hospital with only bruises and cuts, I was afraid to even drive for fear of death. I was under such conviction because of the life I was living that I couldn't wait to run to the altar to ask for forgiveness.

As soon as the church doors opened, I ran to the altar and renewed my faith in Christ. I had never felt better. I stopped drinking and running around with my pot-smoking alcoholic friends. I joined myself with good Christian people but with all that being said I still had the lust of the flesh prodding at me.

As I gained strength, I became active in the ministry and was ordained as a Deacon and then later as an Ordained Baptist Preacher in 1995 even while accommodating the spirit of lust.

The spirit of lust was something the men I confided in said was, 'normal for men to have.' That was a lie!
Before the internet, it was magazines and movies but when the internet came the problem of lusting got bigger.

I was so troubled by Internet pornography I told myself something had to be done. I went to church leaders and they always played it down. They were dealing with the same issues but they would never admit it. They too, had, no idea what to say or do. They too were dealing with their own problems with lust.

I was told by the elders and leaders of several churches that lust was just something you would have to deal with the rest of your life and there was no getting rid of it.

I was told by some that 'lusting after women was just part of a man's life and God put that in us to multiply the earth.' so I partially accepted that and went on living in guilt. I wasn't addicted but I hated the shame and guilt that came with entertaining lust.

As a child of God, you cannot continue to live in sin and get away with it. God chastises those he loves and many times God will do this by exposing your secret sins hoping you will repent and draw closer to Him.

Ephesians 5:11 And do not participate in the unfruitful deeds of darkness, but instead even expose them; for it is disgraceful even to speak of the things which are done by them in secret. But all things become visible when they are exposed by the light, for everything that becomes visible is light.

I was heading for a fall. Years of secretly looking at pornography, flirting, manipulating and lying were about to be exposed— and I knew it. I would blame God by saying, *"You're God and You can stop me." "I've asked You God to deliver me and You're not doing anything to stop it, I can't do this, why aren't You helping me?"*

As a Pastor today, I find in many counseling sessions that the majority of people seeking help blame God and not Satan. They ask God for direction over and over and all the while He's given them directions to follow right in front of them.

The Bible contains all the answers already spoken by God to man and then onto paper. The answers are right there, in God's already spoken word, we just have to look for them. One of the most effective verses is St. Matt 18:18 and learning how to bind or loose these evil spirits but in my early years I had no idea what this verse truly meant.

I would visit churches hoping to find someone who knew how to get set free. You see, I wasn't just satisfied with allowing this sin to remain. I knew God loved me and He knew that I loved Him but I also knew there was more for me. I knew I was hearing God's voice; I could be set free!

I would pray for the preachers on TV and at church to please say something that would help me get set free from these lustful torments. All the while, holding in my hand all of the answers of deliverance in a book called the Holy Bible.

My eyes were opened even more by faith and it was faith that caused me to see. I hungered for more knowledge about deliverance. I began to pray for the Holy Spirit to send me a Christian Brother to teach me more about deliverance.

Remember, I was an ordained minister and was riddled with guilt and shame. I was desperate and crying out from the depths of despair. I wanted to be a holy vessel for God.

2 Timothy 2: 21& 22 *Therefore, if a man cleanses himself from these things, he will be a vessel for honor, sanctified, useful to the Master, prepared for every good work. Now flee from youthful lusts, and pursue righteousness, faith, love and peace, with those who call on the Lord from a pure heart.*

There was one-man God led me to, and he led me to a deeper understanding of the mercy and grace of our Heavenly Father. The man who helped me was Denny Brogan. Denny who was over 20 years older, had dealt with the same thing and had been delivered from the lust of the flesh. He was the first man who ever took the time to listen to my heart. Denny a very laid-back brother in Christ so it was like no big deal to him. He was like, alright this thing has to go, let's go pray it out. I couldn't believe how calm and cool he was, later I found out that it was his faith in the power and authority in the name of Jesus. I asked him, when can we meet to take the battle to the spirit of lust? He later called me and worked out a plan.

After losing to lust since I was 11 years old, in 2003 Denny and I took a stand against my demons on his houseboat on Norris Lake. I told Denny I wasn't coming off this houseboat until the demons of lust were gone. We began by casting down the imaginations and everything that exalted itself above the knowledge of God and tore down the strongholds of lust in my mind in Jesus Name, the battle was on!

He allowed the Holy Spirit to speak through him and for an hour I was being set free from every demon that had ever tormented me.

When we were through, I couldn't believe the freedom I felt. The chains of lust had been broken and I was emptied out of these filthy wicked spirits. I knew it! I just knew it was true! And there I was, filled with great joy and a new outlook on life. There is power in the name of Jesus!

Everywhere I went there wasn't the urge to take a second look and I saw women as sisters instead of objects of my desire. Part of my flesh had died on that cold day in March 2003 but what was really different? I had control over lust instead of it having control over me!

Rom 6:6 *tells us that the persons we used to be were "nailed to the cross with Jesus."*

Romans 6:7 *tells us that "sin does not have power over dead people"*

Romans 13:14 "*Instead clothe yourself with the presence of the Lord Jesus Christ. And don't let yourself think about ways to indulge your evil desires.*"

Please I beg you to repent and stop trying to protect a demon of lust whose whole plan is to destroy you. There's coming a day — because it came upon me — when the Holy Spirit tells your spouse or your parents what you're doing and they will confront you about. Are you willing to lie to protect a demon for the sake of this sinful pleasure?

How many lies are you willing to tell them? How many jobs are you willing to lose because of your lust problem?

God sees you and has witnessed what you've done, what you're doing and what you're about to do. You can't lie to God. He sees all and knows all. Go ahead and confess your sin. I promise the Holy Spirit will teach you how to take control.

1 John 1:9 If we confess our sins, he is faithful and just to forgive us our sins, and to cleanse us from all unrighteousness.
If you worship anything other than God it's idolatry.
An idol can be real or not real.

Definition of Idol: An image or anything (person or thing) used as an object of worship in place of the one and only true God.

Lust and Pride are liars and Jesus is the **"...way, the truth and the life..."**

Tear down those places of sinful worship (also secret places) and idols (statues, pictures, posters) in your home and throw away those sinful magazines, movies, toys and delete those erotic pictures and downloads you think you have protected under a password. Destroy the old black book, Ouija boards, tarot cards, buddhas', yoga practices, social media friends you have hidden must go. Sever yourself from these sources of evil. If you don't, you will continue to struggle.

***Ephesians* 4:21-23** *Since you have heard about Jesus and have learned the truth that comes from him, throw off your old sinful nature and your former way of life, which is corrupted by lust and deception. Instead, let the Spirit renew your thoughts and attitudes.*

Dr. Cole says "Obedience to God's commands brings peace. Peace is heavenly. Only obedience can bring peace. Disobedience shatters peace. God commands confession. Confession to get rid of sin, and confession to put on righteousness. Unconfessed sin is unforgiven sin."

***James* 1: 15** *Then when lust has conceived, it gives birth to sin; and when sin is accomplished, it brings forth death.*

Chapter 2

TO WIN, YOU MUST BE BORN AGAIN

You absolutely have no hope to win against lust without being saved or knowing Jesus as your Savior.

Ephesians 6: 10 – 12 Finally, my brethren, be strong in the Lord, and in the power of his might. Put on the whole armor of God, that ye may be able to stand against the wiles of the devil. For we wrestle not against flesh and blood, but against <u>principalities</u>, against <u>powers</u>, against the <u>rulers of the darkness of this world</u>, against <u>spiritual wickedness in high places.</u>

As Satan is the head of all evil, the next three principalities under Satan carry out his evil commands. Who are they? The **lust of the flesh**, the **lust of the eyes** and the **pride of life**.

We will go deeper into this study in Chapter 3 but right now I want to establish a solid foundation before we move forward in revealing more of God's word to you.

We must start out building our lives upon a good solid foundation. This solid foundation must be built upon a rock. What rock?

St. Matthew 7: 24 – 27 Therefore whosoever heareth these sayings of mine, and doeth them, I will liken him unto a wise man, which built his house upon a rock (Jesus): And the rain descended, and the floods came, and the winds blew, and beat upon that house; and it fell not: for it was founded upon a rock. And every one that heareth these sayings of mine, and doeth them not, shall be likened unto a foolish man, which built his house upon the sand (Satan/World): And the rain descended, and the floods came, and the winds blew, and beat upon that house; and it fell: and great was the fall of it.

Again, your life <u>must be built upon the rock (Jesus)</u> in order to overcome the spirit of lust.

At this time, you may be in a literal prison but more so in two prisons at the same time (a natural one & a spiritual one). From one of those prisons you can be pardoned today. Which one is that? The one in the spiritual realm.
The conditions of the spiritual prison are far worse than any prison man has ever created. This spiritual prison of sinful torments is supernaturally manufactured to mutilate and tear away any hope you may have in God — if any.

Those around you may have no idea what to say to you to help you get set free from the spiritual prison but I know someone who does know how. You may be the one who has some control over lust and pride but you are dangerously close to losing all control.

You may even be the one with complete control over lust and pride but someone you love may be in trouble and needs help now! You've searched for counselors; you've searched for psychiatrists. You went to the church for help but, no one could help you or you didn't have enough money to pay for the help.

I've got great news for you! Deliverance is free! Yes, deliverance is free and you can start today!

Not knowing how to stop a runaway train is terrifying but knowing is half the battle. Not knowing leads many to suicide, self-destruction and many other dangerous behaviors. Knowing leads to restoration and deliverance. When you feel that there's no more hope, the evil voices in your mind rationalize and justify a reason to end it all but the still small voice from the spirit of God gives hope to the brokenhearted and sets the captives free.

When you hear evil voices come into your mind these evil voices (which come from demons) will give you many reasons to sin and even end your life. Have you ever thought of suicide or even hurting yourself? These voices come from evil spirits not you. They say things like:

"You're a looser, and no one will miss you."; "No one cares if you live or die"; "It would be better for us if you just killed yourself"; "You'll never amount to anything so go ahead and do it"; "You're better off in hell. God doesn't love you, how could God love somebody like you"; "Your Dad/Mom was right, you're a piece of crap and wished you had never been born"; "You're ugly and always will be, so, end it for all for us".

More than people would like to admit, people wake up with these evil voices screaming these lies from morning till night. These evil spirits will not stop until you're dead. Every kind of drug man can offer will not stop them until you reach out and seek help in a Deliverance Ministry.

Ask a Psychiatrist their success rate in treating mentally ill patients being totally healed by medication and hospitalization. None according to Professional Counsellor and former Psychiatrist Mike Smith at Hardcore Christianity.

2 Corinthians 10:5 We are destroying speculations and every lofty thing raised up against the knowledge of God, and we are taking every thought captive to the obedience of Christ,

Below are some good questions:

1.) **How did sin originate?** That's right, from Satan.

2.) **How does Satan distribute sin to all of mankind?** Through other Fallen Angels or Demons that tempt us. Once we're tempted, we have a choice to say yes or no. Once the temptation has been manifested into sin our flesh and soul along with the help of demons continue to carry out this sin.

3.) **When did sin start in mankind?** We've been corrupted from the fall of Adam & Eve in the garden of Eden (Genesis 3). You may say, I'm born again, I can't have demons! Wrong, you're still made of three parts (Body, Soul & Spirit) 1 Thessalonians 5:23.

4.) **Can Demons enter Christians?** Yes, through the body and soul. Even today, Christians flood the hospitals around the world seeking help in their body and souls through medication. The Soul controls the mind, will and emotions and the body(flesh) follows.

5.) **Where does the Holy Spirit dwell in you after Salvation through Jesus Christ?** Yes, in your spirit man. This leaves your body and soul exposed to sin and demonic torment. This is why Christians must read and follow through with Ephesians 6th chapter.

6.) **Can Demons possess a Christian?** No. Jesus bought and paid for you and the Holy Spirit lives in your spirit man. Demons can enter the body and soul of Christians but not the spirit man (inner man). Every day around the world demons enter into the body and soul through diseases, mental illnesses, lust, pride, etc. How did they enter? Doors are opened through TV, the Internet, books, magazines, other people, events, etc.

7.) **Can Demons possess an unsaved person?** Yes. To the fullest. Demons will take total possession of a person who has not been saved by grace through faith in Jesus Christ. An unsaved person has **NO** defense against demonic attack or possession.

8.) **Why do demons want to use us?** First, they hate us because we look like God. Second, they're without a fleshly body and they need a fleshly body and soul to carry out their wickedness. Their appetites are filled through the human body and through the lustful activities that humans get involved in.

*St. Matthew 12:43 – 45 When the unclean spirit is gone out of man, he walketh through dry places, seeking rest, and finds none. Then he saith, I will return into my house **(person's body)** from whence I came out; and when he is come, he finds it empty, swept, and **garnished (when demons leave the body, you're at peace and cleaned up)**. Then goeth he, and taketh with himself seven other spirits more wicked than himself, and they enter in and dwell there: and the last state of that man is worse than the first. Even so shall it be also unto this wicked generation.*

Your only hope of deliverance from this world and from the powers of the enemy is through Jesus Christ. You may have heard it a thousand times or you may have never heard it all— but, Jesus really and truly loves you and He really is the only way (St. John 14:6). It's this genuine love that draws people from every nation to Christ Jesus.

You may not even believe love exists but that doesn't change the fact love does exist in the person of Jesus Christ. You have free will to receive it or not! If you do receive His love please don't do it out of fear of Satan and his demons but out of God's love that's drawing you to Jesus now.

Even after salvation, that same love and hope we get from Jesus will be the same hope and love that will deliver you time and time again throughout your life. Why confess Jesus as your Lord? Because he's the key person in your rescue attempt.

Jesus is the only one who can find you in this desperate wilderness of life. A wilderness with no trails or guideposts except for One. The One whose footsteps you hear coming closer in a wilderness you thought you would die in. He knows how to find you and where to find you. His name is Jesus. Will you accept him into your life today?

Please say yes to Jesus.

Romans 10:9 *Confess with thy mouth the Lord Jesus and believe in thy heart that God raised him from the dead and thou shalt be saved.*

If you don't accept Jesus into your life now, my hope is for you to do so by the end of this book.

Why is salvation so important to overcome the lust of the flesh, the lust of the eyes and the pride of life?

Because it's salvation and the baptism of the Holy Spirit that gives you the power over Satan and all of his evil forces.

You may be saying, "the last thing that I want is Jesus in my life. Christians ain't nothing but a bunch of hypocrites and the churches are filled with nothing but a bunch of liars and whoremongers.

The very people who told you about Jesus may be the ones you blame to this day about your problems.

They may be the ones who crammed the Bible down your throat while they themselves were slaves to sin.

They sorely misrepresented the love of God, so now you want nothing to do with God because of them.

You may even proudly boast that you're not a hypocrite like these ole backslidden Christians but, inside you're a mess and this anger you've had for them has eaten a hole in your soul.

Anger has led you right into the arms of Rebellion and Rejection and these strong spirits do not play nice. The Rejection of the Father/Mother, Husband/Wife, Children/Grandchildren will cause rebellion against God.

Do you really want to deny salvation all because of those who hurt you?

Someday whether you believe it or not you will kneel at the Great White Throne Judgement in great fear. Some people think they're going to give God a piece of their mind, not so. Trembling before the son of God and the Creator of all mankind, you'll listen to your final judgment for the life you've lived right before you're thrown into a lake a fire. Harsh words but— true!

Pointing fingers and bitterness against the ones who hurt you will not work at the Great White Throne Judgment.

Revelation 20: 11-15 And I saw a great white throne, and him that sat on it, from whose face the earth and the heaven fled away; and there was found no place for them. And I saw the dead, small and great, stand before God; and the books were opened: and another book was opened, which is the book of life: and the dead were judged out of those things which were written in the books, according to their works. And the sea gave up the dead which were in it; and death and hell delivered up the dead which were in them: and they were judged every man according to their works. And death and hell were cast into the lake of fire. This is the second death. And whosoever was not found written in the book of life was cast into the lake of fire.

You may be a tough gal or guy here on this earth and you may command respect on this earth but on the other side you'll bow and confess Jesus as Lord of Lords and Kings of Kings.

This is a tough statement but it's filled with love. Love that is so concerned for your eternal well-being and love that could only come from our Heavenly Father to you. It's an urgent call but a loving call.

I would rather rattle your cage now and ask you to humble yourself and repent than to wait until it's too late to turn to Christ after you die.

After you die without Christ, I promise you that you will scream and yell out "I repent!" But it'll be too late. God loves you and it's not by fear God wants you to receive His Son Jesus but by His love. It's His love that draws us to Jesus not the fear of the flames of fire of Hell.

Now, do you want to overcome these giants in your life?

Then the most important step in getting delivered is to repent and ask Jesus to come into your life. It will be the best decision you've ever made. I promise!

Prayer of Salvation

Please, just ask him now:
Jesus, I confess you as Lord and I believe you love me. Please forgive me for all of my sins. I choose you, Jesus, this day and turn from practicing sin. I believe you're the son of God, you died on the cross and that you rose from the grave on the third day. Jesus, I believe in You!

If you said this prayer and believed every word, you're now a new person, born again, saved by the grace of God. Your name has been written into the Book of Life in Heaven. Hallelujah!!!

You're now on the road to victory. The giants are going down!

Chapter 3

Demonic Influences

From the Lust of the Flesh, Lust of the Eyes and the Pride of Life we find demon groupings:

I first heard of demon groupings by listening to teaching by Frank Hammond and Derek Prince. Derek Prince called them *"demon gangs"*. Both of these men, along with Win Worley have witnessed thousands of these demon groupings manifest under Lust and Pride.

These great men have laid the groundwork for many of us deliverance and healing ministers. Even though, all three of these great men have passed away they have left behind many books and teachings worth their weight in gold. That is to say, the books are worth it and then some but the Holy Bible is our greatest resource.

In deliverance here at Freedom Crossing we run into many demon gangs. Below are just a few that have manifested and come out of people.

Here are a few demons that manifested and came out under the strong man of the lust of the flesh:

1.) Celebrity idol worship

2.) Sex Toys (Not mentioning names of them)

3.) Virtual Reality Sex

4.) Sex Robots

5.) Sex Dolls

6.) Pedophilia

7.) Multiple Partners

8.) Fetishes

9.) Bestiality

10.) Fornication

11.) Adultery

12.) Masturbation

13.) Oral Sex

14.) Same Sex

15.) Bondage

Here are a few demons that manifested and came out under the lust of the eyes:

1.) Certain Kinds of Food

2.) Cars

3.) Trucks

4.) Houses

5.) Money

6.) Power

7.) Fame

8.) Land

9.) Airplanes

10.) Self-Image Worship
11.) Religious Idol Worship
12.) People
13.) Drinks
14.) Jewelry
15.) Clothes

Here are a few that manifested and came out under the pride of life:

1.) Boasting
2.) Cocky or Arrogant
3.) Domination
4.) Rebellion
5.) Cold
6.) Selfish/Vain
7.) Narcissist
8.) Unaffectionate
9.) Conditional Love
10.) Multiple Marriages
11.) Degradation of Others
12.) Poor Loser
13.) Trophy Chaser
14.) Stubborn
15.) Prideful

In 2 Sam 12 1:15 we see how demon groupings work together to destroy a man. As you read the scripture, you'll notice I've typed in who Nathan is identifying in his story to David. You may be surprised.

12 *Then the* LORD *sent Nathan to David. And he came to him and said,*

"There were two men (David & Uriah) in one city, the one rich and the other poor.

2 "The rich man (David) had a great many flocks (wives) and herds (concubines).

3 "But the poor man (Uriah) had nothing except one little ewe lamb (Bethsheba his wife) which he bought and nourished; And it grew up together with him and his children. It would eat of his bread and drink of his cup and lie in his bosom, And was like a daughter to him.

4 "Now a traveler (Adultery) came to the rich man (David), And he was unwilling to take from his own flock (wives) or his own herd (concubines), To prepare for the wayfarer (Adultery needs another man's wife to accomplish sin) who had come to him; Rather he took the poor man's ewe lamb (Bethsheba) and prepared it for the man (Adultery) who had come to him."

5 Then David's anger burned greatly against the man (About to find out that it was himself), and he said to Nathan, "As the LORD lives, surely the man who has done this deserves to die.

⁶ He must make restitution for the lamb fourfold, because he did this thing and had no compassion."

⁷ Nathan then said to David, "You are the man (rich man)! Thus, says the LORD God of Israel, 'It is I who anointed you king over Israel and it is I who delivered you from the hand of Saul.

⁸ I also gave you your master's house and your master's wives into your care, and I gave you the house of Israel and Judah; and if that had been too little, I would have added to you many more things like these!

⁹ Why have you despised the word of the LORD by doing evil in His sight? You have struck down Uriah the Hittite with the sword, have taken his wife to be your wife, and have killed (spirit of murder) him with the sword of the sons of Ammon.

¹⁰ Now therefore, the sword shall never depart from your house (curse came through David's sin), because you have despised Men (spirit of rebellion) and have taken the wife of Uriah the Hittite to be your wife.'

¹¹ Thus says the LORD, 'Behold, I will raise up evil against you from your own household; I will even take your wives (spirit of division and theft) before your eyes and give them to your companion, and he will lie with your wives in broad daylight (Adultery turned on David and used David's own son Absalom to rape 10 of David's concubines).

¹² *Indeed you did it secretly, but I will do this thing before all Israel, and under the sun.'"*

¹³ *Then David said to Nathan, "I have sinned against the LORD." And Nathan said to David, "The LORD also has taken away your sin; you shall not die.*

¹⁴ *However, because by this deed you have given occasion to the enemies of the LORD to blaspheme, the child also that is born to you shall surely die"* (Spirit of death came on the innocent because of David's sin).

¹⁵ *So Nathan went to his house.*

How many other demon groupings did you see in this story?

_____

_____

_____

_____

Chapter 4

The Big Three Trouble Makers

<u>1 John 2:16 & 17</u> *For all that is in the world, the **lust of the flesh**, and the **lust of the eyes**, and the **pride of life**, is not of the Father, but is of the world." Verse 17 "and the world passes away, and the lust thereof: but he that doeth the will of God abides forever.*

Who are these Big Three Trouble Makers?
   1.) Lust of the Eyes
   2.) Lust of the Flesh
   3.) Pride of Life

Some of you may be saying why give them credit by identifying them as the "Big Three". Ok, fair enough. How about the big three dummies, no that won't work because they're very intelligent, they're actually masterminds of evil.

How about "The little three"? No, that won't do because they've all three caused the biggest problems in the history of mankind under Satan's authority.

Satan has many evil principalities working in our world today. One of those principalities is soon to come in a man called the Anti-Christ. The Anti-Christ will be filled with the Big Three and more.

Revelations 13: 1 – 10 And I stood upon the sand of the sea, and saw a beast rise up out of the sea, having seven heads and ten horns, and upon his horns ten crowns, and upon his heads the name of blasphemy. And the beast which I saw was like unto a leopard, and his feet were as the feet of a bear, and his mouth as the mouth of a lion: and the dragon gave him his power, and his seat, and great authority. And I saw one of his heads as it were wounded to death; and his deadly wound was healed: and all the world wondered after the beast. And they worshipped the dragon which gave power unto the beast: and they worshipped the beast, saying, Who is like unto the beast? who is able to make war with him? And there was given unto him a mouth speaking great things and blasphemies; and power was given unto him to continue forty and two months. And he opened his mouth in blasphemy against God, to blaspheme his name, and his tabernacle, and them that dwell in heaven.

And it was given unto him to make war with the saints, and to overcome them: and power was given him over all kindreds, and tongues, and nations. And all that dwell upon the earth shall worship him, whose names are not written in the book of life of the Lamb slain from the foundation of the world. If any man has an ear, let him hear. He that leadeth into captivity shall go into captivity: he that killeth with the sword must be killed with the sword. Here is the patience and the faith of the saints.

Rejection and Rebellion.

God or Abba (Daddy/Papa) Father is our all-time greatest ally and Satan and his punk demons know it. What better way to get you away from Papa God than to send in the wolves of rejection and rebellion after you have opened the door to lusts and pride?

<u>**Here's how they work**</u>:

1.) Rebellion & Rejection come through the family tree through verbal abuse, sexual abuse, abortion, orphans (unwanted), through witchcraft, mediums and all occultic activities, Father not at home, lack of love from the Father, etc.

2.) Rebellion ushers in witchcraft, mediums, sorcery, adultery, fornication, Jezebel and mind control spirits. After the sinful act of participating with these evil spirits, the spirit of rejection comes which in turn brings with it self-rejection, cutting, rage, physical abuse, suicide and much more.

3.) With lust of the flesh after the orgasm or a fleshly/soulish high the evil spirit of guilt and condemnation comes in. They wreak havoc on the Christians of this world through pornography, alcoholism, prescription drugs, street drugs, video games, gambling and many forms of sex and sinful highs and lows. Bringing great amounts of guilt and shame into their lives.

4.) After the evil highs and lows then comes anger, depression, loneliness, fighting, arguing, hatred, hurt, criticism, cruelty and abuse. In which all of these are evil spirits.

5.) Then more of Rejection. Rejection ushers in more serious evil spirits: suicide, overdoses, crime, imprisonment, despair, insomnia, gloom, anxiety, dread, schizophrenia, body dysmorphic disorder, anorexia, bulimia, etc.

This is a basic general overview of the workings of lust of the eyes, lust of the flesh and the pride of life through rejection and rebellion.

And you thought you were only battling yourself all of this time. Not so!

You were created in God's image and you were created as a temple for the spirit of God to live in. You're worth the death of Jesus on the cross, yes you are!

Others may have been hard on you but, now that you know who's been wickedly encouraging you to act this way, you're on your way to revealing and conquering these giants (demons) in Christ Jesus name.

Yes, you have to take responsibility for what you've done but that was in the past. Today's a new day!

The Big Three know how to inflict great misery on a human being and when they do, they know how to manipulate you into blaming God. They prey on the strong and the weak and have no problems destroying the rich and the poor.

The Big Three continually send out the wolves of rejection and rebellion to try and make you suppress the pain you feel through drugs, alcohol, sex, and many other evil things.

The spirit of Pride has taught you how to cover the deep soul wounds you've had for years through the use of overeating, sex outside of marriage, alcohol, porn, drugs and avoiding help from the right ministries.

The spirit of pride is carrying out the plans of Satan 24/7 and know that their purpose is "...to kill, steal and destroy."

BUT GOD! Has a wonderful glorious plan for your life! Even behind the bars of a literal or spiritual prison cell you can find that God has a plan for you now, yes now! *Jeremiah 29: 11 – 13 For I know the thoughts that I think toward you, saith the LORD, thoughts of peace, and not of evil, to give you an expected end. Then shall ye call upon me, and ye shall go and pray unto me, and I will hearken unto you. And ye shall seek me, and find me, when ye shall search for me with all your heart.*

All this time, you may have thought that you were just an outcast and a black sheep of the family. WRONG!

In all the families of the world, our ancestors have sinned against God except for one man (Jesus) who came from heaven and was placed in the womb of Mary to be born in human form so he could bear on himself our sins, take them to a cross and shed His blood — the only blood that could redeem us from our own sins.

This man Jesus (our Savior) died but more importantly rose from the grave on the third day victorious over all the powers of sin, Satan, death, hell and the grave.

Jesus said in *St Luke 10: 19 & 20. Behold, I give unto you power to tread on serpents and scorpions, and over all the power of the enemy: and nothing shall by any means hurt you. Notwithstanding in this rejoice not, that the spirits are subject unto you; but rather rejoice, because your names are written in heaven.*

Jesus also said in *St. Mark 16: 17* *And these signs shall follow them that believe; In my name shall they cast out devils; they shall speak with new tongues;*

Because of Jesus, you've been given spiritual weapons to battle against the evil spirits in your life through the power of the Holy Spirit.

2 Corinthians 10: 3 - 5 *For though we walk in the flesh, we do not war after the flesh: (For the weapons of our warfare are not carnal, but mighty through God to the pulling down of strong holds;) Casting down imaginations, and every high thing that exalted itself against the knowledge of God, and bringing into captivity every thought to the obedience of Christ;*

Ephesians 6: 11 & 12 *Put on the whole armor of God, that ye may be able to stand against the wiles of the devil. For we wrestle not against flesh and blood, but against principalities, against powers, against the rulers of the darkness of this world, against spiritual wickedness in high places.*

You see, forget the secular shallow way of treating mental illness, schizophrenia, bi-polar, anxiety and give Jesus a chance to prove his love for you.

St. John 8: 31 – 36 *Then said Jesus to those Jews which believed on him, If ye continue in my word, then are ye my disciples indeed; And ye shall know the truth, and the truth shall make you free. They answered him, we be Abraham's seed, and were never in bondage to any man: how sayest thou, Ye shall be made free?*

Jesus answered them, Verily, verily, I say unto you, Whosoever committeth sin is the servant of sin. And the servant abideth not in the house for ever: but the Son abideth ever. If the Son therefore shall make you free, ye shall be free indeed.

Your ancestors may have dabbled in the occult which is filled with lust and pride of every sort. Since your ancestors took part in these occult practices every child born in your family since then has the curse placed onto them down through the ages all the way to you.

Exodus **34:7** *Who keeps lovingkindness for thousands, who forgives iniquity, transgression and sin; yet He will by no means leave the guilty unpunished, visiting the* ***iniquity of fathers on the children and on the grandchildren to the third and fourth generations.***

So, what are you saying? That the curses of my earthly fathers must be broken? Yes!

All the spells, hexes and vexes that have been spoken over you and your ancestors through witchcraft, sorcery, psychics, fortune tellers, mediums and warlocks have to be broken in the mighty name of Christ Jesus!

How do I break such curses in your life? Let's start with this prayer:

Heavenly Father, I come to you in the name of your son Jesus Christ to break every generational curse that has been placed over me and my family. I ask you Heavenly Father to break every chain, every cord, every tie and every evil word spoken over me in Jesus Name! With the power of the Holy Spirit I come against every evil spirit in my family and in me, and I now bind these evil spirits and loose them out to where Jesus would send them. I evict each and every demon which has ever set up in my body and soul and now place a no trespassing sign upon my temple that is only for my Heavenly Father's use. Dear Jesus, wash me with your blood and clean all of the evil residue left behind from these filthy demons. Amen!

Take a second. What did you sense? Did you cough? Did your body jerk? What emotion did you feel? Did you feel a stirring in a particular part of your mind and body?

If so, then you hit a nerve. And that nerve was one of those trouble makers inside of you.

If you're a Christian, ask the Holy Spirit to help you identify each trouble maker and began by claiming the blood of Jesus over your life and binding and loosing immediately. Demons can't stand the blood of Jesus because the demons can't win over the blood of Jesus. The demons will be forced out by the blood and name of Jesus Christ. Try it! I promise, if you stay on them with the blood of Jesus the trouble makers will have to leave you.

The demons have no problem wearing you down. It's time child of God, that you start wearing them down!

Wear them down with worship, praise and thanksgiving for your deliverance is in the mighty name of JESUS not Dr. TakeYoMoney!

If a stranger comes to your home and all they want to do is cause problems, don't you think you would want to evict them? Some of you immediately would call 911 or some of you would take matters into your own hands.

Well, we have the same authority in the spirit realm. Declare war and fight! Bind and Loose in Jesus's Name!

2 Corinthians 10: 3 – 6 For though we walk in the flesh, we do not war according to the flesh, for the weapons of our warfare are not of the flesh, but divinely powerful for the destruction of fortresses. We are destroying speculations and every lofty thing raised up against the knowledge of God, and we are taking every thought captive to the obedience of Christ, and we are ready to punish all disobedience, whenever your obedience is complete.

Hollywood has painted this picture in our minds that a priest/preacher has to show up with a cross and fling holy water at the person until the demons come out.

Not so, all we need is the name of Jesus to command these evil spirits to come out, we already have the authority through salvation in Christ Jesus.

When the demons come out, they come out in many different ways. Through a cough, yawn, long breath but sometimes they do try to hurt the person as they come out. If this is the case, you'll need other people to help assist you as they hold the person and you continue to command every evil spirit to come out. This process could take less than a minute or it may take hours.

If you have no idea what I'm talking about then that's why you need to come to our fellowship and watch a Deliverance Team in action.

If you live too far away then we'll try to find you a deliverance ministry in your area to help you. Don't take on demons in someone else alone. You'll need an experienced deliverance worker to help you.

You see these demons have been passed down through many generations and our ancestors may have not have known how to stop them. But praise God you're learning how to stop them and learning how to break the generational curses that have been manifesting through you and others for generations. Write the eviction notice today and serve the papers against them!!!

1 Corinthians 3:17 Do you not know that you are a temple of God and that the Spirit of God dwells in you? If any man destroys the temple of God, God will destroy him, for the temple of God is holy, and that is what you are.

Again, some of you still may be saying I'm already a Christian and Christians can't have demons. Pastor, you've lost your mind!

I used to think the same way because of the false doctrines I was taught. I would hear Christian testimonies, "the devil made me do it", "all day the devil was just putting thoughts into my mind," "I saw the devil in that man," and when it comes to casting the devil out of them, "why, a Christian can't have a demon." Lord, help us!

We're made up of a body, soul and spirit. (1 Thessalonians 5:23)

When you become a Christian the spirit of God or the Holy Spirit comes to dwell in your spirit man not your body and soul.

Your body and soul is still susceptible to the attacks of demons. Our soul controls the mind, will and emotions so how many Christians do you know with some serious mental problems? A few, right!

How many Christians do you know who have died of cancer, heart attack, kidney disease and so on? God didn't create these diseases, Satan did and these diseases enter the body through demons who specialize in causing these illnesses. We've witnessed these demons come out of people in deliverance & healing services and go back to the doctor and find no trace of that disease or problem in them.

Through sin, came sickness and infirmities but the only way to defeat sin that brought death is to receive life which is through Jesus Christ.

Yes, the body will perish but your soul & spirit will live on. Live on where? Well that's up to you. You have a choice of two places: Heaven or Hell. Hell is the easiest choice because it requires you to do nothing but live life your way and not God's way.

Choose Heaven and forfeit your life and, in turn give your life to Jesus. He, in turn, freely gives you more than hell could ever offer. Hell offers torments and pain forever but Heaven offers love and joy forever. It's your choice.

Do you want to fight and I mean *fight* against Satan and all the lies he's told you for years? Then come against the spirit of lust and pride with the gifts of the Holy Spirit. *1 Corinthians 12: 8-10*.

These gifts along with the authority of the word of God will crush every stronghold the enemy has ever built in your mind. You're heading for freedom if you use the word of God as a weapon against Satan. *St. Matthew 4: 1-11*.

All too often Christians will go through deliverance and will get set free of all the demons but go back into the old routine of life and open the same doors the other demons came through.

After deliverance it's imperative you study the Bible and spend time with God, Jesus and the Holy Spirit. It's of the utmost importance that you remain in fellowship with a body of believers who are sold out to Jesus. If you can't find a group of believers in your area then watch us on YouTube or move closer to Clinton, TN. Everyone is welcome and we're not afraid to come against any problem you may have in Jesus Name.

We love every human being but please stay away from Catholic priests, money-hungry ministry workers and cults. Mormons, Jehovah Witnesses, Masons or any other secret society are a false man-made denomination. These folks will make your life worse. The gospel of Jesus is an open book and to join the family of God is open to all to and nothing is secret.

When Jesus set up the church, He intended for everyone to be united in love. Man needed more control so the spirit of pride started to divide one church body from the other. This attitude about your denomination being the only way, has got to go.

This may anger you but these evil spirits have some control over you when you become part of something Jesus himself didn't approve of. You'll never know what I'm talking about until you leave your denomination. It's part of your deliverance and the freedom is wonderful!

When born again through Christ we become Christians and nothing more. Christians unite under one Head, Christ Jesus! Deliverance is your step in the right direction.

Deliverance and casting out demons still may seem foreign to you. You may have never been shown in the word of God the many instances of demons being cast out of people.

Let's go back and take a look at what Jesus said when he rebuked Peter. Peter was born again and you can't be born again unless the spirit of God dwells in you. But we see in this instance where Satan came into Peter and spoke through him.

St. Matthew **16: 21-23** *From that time forth began Jesus to shew unto his disciples, how that he must go unto Jerusalem, and suffer many things of the elders and chief priests and scribes, and be killed, and be raised again the third day. Then Peter took him, and began to rebuke him, saying, be it far from thee, Lord: this shall not be unto thee. But he (Jesus) turned and said unto Peter, **<u>get thee behind me, Satan: thou art an offence unto me: for thou sourest not the things that be of God, but those that be of men.</u>***

Another instance of a man becoming a Christian and soon after a spirit of bitterness entered him.

Acts 8: 13 – 24 *Then Simon himself believed also: and when he was baptized, he continued with Philip, and wondered, beholding the miracles and signs which were done.*

Now when the apostles which were at Jerusalem heard that Samaria had received the word of God, they sent unto them Peter and John: Who, when they were come down, prayed for them, that they might receive the Holy Ghost: (For as yet he was fallen upon none of them: only they were baptized in the name of the Lord Jesus.) Then laid they their hands on them, and they received the Holy Ghost. And when Simon saw that through laying on of the apostles' hands the Holy Ghost was given, he offered them money, Saying, Give me also this power, that on whomsoever I lay hands, he may receive the Holy Ghost. But Peter said unto him, thy money perish with thee, because thou hast thought that the gift of God may be purchased with money. Thou hast neither part nor lot in this matter: for thy heart is not right in the sight of God. Repent therefore of this thy wickedness, and pray God, if perhaps the *thought of thine heart may be forgiven thee. For I perceive that thou art **in the gall of bitterness, and in the bond of iniquity**. Then answered Simon, and said, pray ye to the Lord for me, that none of these things which ye have spoken come upon me.*

This man (Simon) in Acts 8th chapter got saved and then saw Peter and John laying their hands on someone and receiving the baptism of the Holy Spirit. Simon wanted that power through the giving of money. Bitterness is an evil spirit which will eat at a man and cause pre-mature death. Peter recognized this spirit in Simon and rebuked the spirit in Simon.

Chapter 5

Lusty

I included this message because it has been the one message everyone remembers the most. You're welcome to use it. I took a puppet with arms and legs and wrote Lusty on a shirt and put him into my object lesson one Sunday morning. Lusty had pink spiky hair and was about four feet tall. He looked cute but was far from cute— his name said it all.

The message goes as follows.
Today, I'll be preaching on LUST! I'm not going to preach on every aspect and every scripture in the Bible on Lust because the Holy Spirit wants me to keep this message as plain and narrow as possible.
Let's get started.

There are 3 Forms of Lust: Lust of Flesh, Lust of Eyes and the Pride of Life; we find these in 1 John 2:16&17

1 John 2:16 & 17 For all that is in the world, the lust of the flesh, and the lust of the eyes, and the pride of life, is not of the Father, but is of the world." Verse 17 "and the world passes away, and the lust thereof: but he that doeth the will of God abides forever.

Men & Women listen!

2 Timothy 2:22 Run from anything that stimulates youthful lusts. Instead, pursue righteous living, faithfulness, love, and peace. Enjoy the companionship of those who call on the Lord with pure hearts.

Lust was created and crafted by Satan and distributed out by his filthy demons.

It didn't just show up out of nowhere. Satan tempted Eve with Lust of the eyes in the Garden of Eden. Eve and Adam ate the fruit because it looked good and would cause them to become like God.

Satan knows the desires of mankind and will test and prod you until he finds a weakness and then strikes.

When Lust has been passed down from generation to generation, people and families are willing to lie and even kill to protect it. Generational curse after generational curse leads families to protect and defend their relationship with lust.

Fathers have taught their sons and sons have taught their sons how to lust for women, money, power and fame and like a cancer lust infects generations of people.

Romans 6:23 For the wages of sin is death; but the gift of God is eternal life through Jesus Christ our Lord.

Let's dig deeper into the tragedies of Lust.

One of the greatest tragedies in the world today is the desensitizing of mankind through pornography. Viewing porn is as easy as accessing drinking water for some.

A man or a woman addicted to pornography will labor to find time for this sinful habit. Spending hours fantasizing and chatting to people around the world.

What is this great porn tragedy producing?

Here are some statistics on adult interaction with pornography:

- *Men admitting to accessing porn at work:* **20%**

- *US adults who regularly visit Internet pornography websites:* **40 million**

- *Christians who said pornography is a major problem in the home:* **47%**

- *Adults admitting to Internet sexual addiction:* **10%**

- **13%** *of women admit to accessing porn at work*

- **70%** *of women keep their cyber activities secret*

- **17%** *of all women struggle with porn addiction*

- *Women favor chat rooms* **2x** *more than men.*

- *1 of 3 visitors of all adult web sites is a woman.*

- *Years of viewing porn causing the heterosexual man or woman to start admiring the same sex instead of the other. Thus, causing the viewer to become a homosexual.*

Almost all of the men and women who were caught by police in sexually related criminal acts admitted to being addicted to porn. Lust uses porn to fuel the desire for more — never satisfied with the same and always thinking about yourself.

What is porn doing to the covenant of marriage?

God intended sex for the covenant of marriage.

God intended for a man to be attracted to a woman and a woman to be attracted to a man. And God intended for the husband and wife to have sex inside the covenant of a Biblical marriage. God told Adam and Eve to be fruitful and multiply, not Adam and Steve. Adam and Steve can't reproduce another human being. Only a male & female can produce another human being.

God made our bodies to produce chemicals which are released when excited by each other. When these chemicals are released in a Holy loving way in marriage the results are amazing.

When these chemicals (endorphins, hormones, etc.) are released during sinful pleasures such as porn, adultery, fornication and fantasies leading to masturbation the results bring on more sin. Such as, depression, loneliness, anger, frustration, worry, disease, premature death.

We must understand that lust is not love!

Here's a few definitions of Lust: unbridled sexual desire; to have an intense desire; an intense longing.

Lust is sin and is never Holy. There's no such thing as Holy Lust. **Lust is not love, but here's what love is!**

In the beginning of a Godly relationship your desire should be to love the other person as Christ loves the church. Even years into the relationship your respect and honor for them should grow. True love for someone will cause you to be excited about loving them unconditionally each and every day.

1 Corinthians 13:4-7 *Love is patient and kind. Love is not jealous or boastful or proud or rude. It does not demand its own way. It is not irritable, and it keeps no record of being wronged.* **(Look at your neighbor on both sides of you and tell them I'm keeping no records of your wrongs).**

Verse 6 It does not rejoice about injustice but rejoices whenever the truth wins out.

Verse 7 Love never gives up, never loses faith, is always hopeful, and endures through every circumstance.

1 Corithians 14:1 *Let love be your* **highest goal**! *But you should also desire the special abilities the Spirit gives – especially the ability to prophesy.*

The world has taught many of us that lust should win over before love.

I've heard women and men alike tell me "Well, I want to sleep with them first before I marry them.", "Maybe I won't like them after I sleep with them."

Lust, then marriage, is destructive. But love then marriage is holy. Repeat!

Porn, soft porn, and almost porn on your computers and your phones are replacing the intimate times you should be having with your spouses.

Lust is such a big part of your life you carry it around and wear it all over you. It's obvious to anyone that knows you; lust is in control of your life because of what comes out of your mouth and how you look at other women or how some women look at men.

Week after week so many men and women live secret lives filled with lust—so I've brought in a so-called friend to help me with an object lesson today.

His name is Lusty. Lusty represents the Spirit of Lust (lust of the eyes, lust of the flesh & pride of life).

Acting out Scene 1:
In House. When you (woman or man) close that door to your room and the computer goes on you may have your parents or your spouse fooled but God sees everything.
Act out a skit with lusty (not intending to be funny) Lusty is on your back with arms across your shoulder. After the family leaves for the grocery store, you go to the computer with Lusty on your back. Act like you're watching porn but the spouse forgot something and has come back unnoticed. Then act as if you are about to be caught.

The spouse sees you and you try to wiggle your way out and lie to protect Lusty. All the while, Lusty's arms are wrapped around your neck and hanging on your back.

Scene 2:
At Work. Act out a flirtation relationship with female/male because Porn isn't enough anymore. You need more and you believe an affair will fill that void. She/he invites you to her/his place and you go tagging Lusty along. Walk off stage as if you're opening a door and going into her/his house.

Scene 3:
In altar trying to repent. Lusty is trying to get me to leave the altar and keeps saying lust is normal and God said it was ok. Lusty wants me to believe a lie.

Have someone pray over me and all the while I have lusty on my back and push him off when I raise up. When I walk away, I don't notice but he's still tied to me (with a string). I didn't truly surrender; I only was humanly sorrowful and remorseful for my actions but didn't repent with a Godly sorrow that leads to true repentance.

I walk away defeated dragging Lusty behind me.
I come back without Lusty and explain what Lust has done and will do to you if not dealt with.

Many Christian men/women are in this condition as I just portrayed on stage. Many Christians find themselves in the altar every Sunday and have never truly cut the ties of lust off of them. It's time to get serious about cutting ties with lust and allow Jesus Christ to wash you and deliver you from the tormentors.

Acts 17:30 And the times of this ignorance God winked at; but now God commands all men everywhere to repent.

God didn't invite me to repent but <u>**commanded me**</u> to repent. He didn't say to me I love and understand your problem. He said I command all men everywhere to repent! I know you should repent because when you get caught, you're going to be wishing you had.

These are some things that happen when people get caught in lustful activities such as murder, rage, divorce, abuse and so on. This is an opportune time for more demon groupings to manifest.

1.) If caught, some get mad at the spouse, the parent, a friend and blame them for their sin. They'll admit their sin but blame others.

2.) Some are sorry once they're caught but, they're afraid to get help because of the shame that comes with it.

3.) Some will feel relieved and come and repent no matter what the consequences.

4.) Some will lie no matter if they have been caught in the very act. It will always be somebody else's fault. They will never admit to it even when the evidence is before them.

Edwin Louis Cole said, "Human sorrow is when we are only sorry for getting caught. Godly sorrow is when we are sorry for the sin, and have a desire to be rid of it."

Remember, one of the sinful partners of lust is the "pride of life". Pride will cause you not to repent or even admit you have a problem. Pride is the opposite of being humble and of a contrite spirit.

Pro 16:18 Pride goes before destruction, a haughty(arrogant) spirit before a fall. You're heading for a fall if you don't humbly repent today.

Chapter 6

Prayers of Deliverance

Psalm 91: 1 He who dwells in the shelter of the Most High will abide in the shadow of the Almighty.

Please make Psalm 91:1 one of your all-time favorites. If you put into practice living in the shelter and shadow of the Almighty you will overcome every obstacle placed in your way by the enemy. If you waver and begin to live outside the shadow of the Almighty you will experience defeat after defeat.

I encourage you to memorize this prayer Jesus taught his disciples to pray:

St. Matthew 6:9-13 *After this manner therefore pray ye: Our Father which art in heaven, Hallowed be thy name. Thy kingdom come. Thy will be done in earth, as it is in heaven. Give us this day our daily bread. And forgive us our debts, as we forgive our debtors. And lead us not into temptation, but deliver us from evil: For thine is the kingdom, and the power, and the glory, forever. Amen. For if ye forgive men their trespasses, your heavenly Father will also forgive you: But if ye forgive not men their trespasses, neither will your Father forgive your trespasses.*

One of my all-time favorite prayers is this one written by my great friend, Pastor Roy Ellis.

"A Prayer of Deliverance" (Written by Pastor Roy Ellis)

I pray, Heavenly Father in the name of our Lord and Savior Jesus Christ. I do first affirm and believe that Jesus Christ is the Son of the living God. I also, affirm and believe that this same Jesus died on the cross for my sins and was raised from the dead that I might have eternal life. I also, affirm and believe that through the blood of Jesus Christ that I'm saved, sanctified, glorified, made righteous and set free. I do affirm and believe that through the blood of Jesus Christ and by the word of my testimony that I have been made an overcomer over all of the powers of the enemy.

I therefore, apply the blood of Jesus Christ to all areas of my life and my family's lives. I apply the blood of Jesus Christ to my body, my soul, my spirit, my mind, my will, my senses, my emotions my conscience and my subconscious mind. That I might bring every thought into captivity to the obedience of Christ and to the glory of God the Father. I apply the blood of Jesus Christ to my children and their families, to my grandchildren, to my mother, my father, my sisters, my brothers and all other family members on both sides of the family tree.

I ask the Father to renew and restore my mind through the washing of the water by the word of God, through the anointing of God by the Holy Spirit and by the blood of Jesus Christ. That He would create in me a clean heart and renew a right spirit within me so that I would have the mind of Christ working in and through my life.

I also forgive and ask forgiveness for the sins of anyone who has ever hurt me, living or dead either by accident or design. I release them into the loving mercy of the Father and I cover them with the blood of Jesus Christ. I also ask the Father to forgive my sins that I'm aware of or might not be aware of so that nothing would stand between us. I ask the Father for a fresh anointing of the Holy Spirit and for that fresh anointing to be poured over my mind, my body, my soul and my spirit so that it would break all bonds, chains, yokes, strongholds and all other evil powers from the enemy in my life.

I proclaim that by the blood of Jesus Christ and the anointing of God through the Holy Spirit that I have the victory over all demons and demonic forces in the spirit realm; kings, rulers of this world, principalities, powers of darkness in this world and against spiritual wickedness in high places and over all other powers of the enemy.

I ask the Father to send His Holy angels to place a hedge of protection around myself and my family. I ask the Father by the Holy Spirit to show me the way that I should walk and to guide me in every area of my life. I ask the Father through the Holy Spirit to increase (in my life) all of the gifts, fruits of the Spirit and especially the gift of spiritual discernment with the fruit of love.

I proclaim that by the blood of Jesus Christ and the anointing of the Holy Spirit that I have broken every generational curse that has been passed down or placed upon either side of my family.

I break every demonic ungodly soul tie in my life and in my family's lives. I break every plague of sickness, injuries in my body, soul, spirit, or anything else that is not of God in my life or in my family's lives. I also break any and all spells, hexes, vexes, jinxes and curses. I break the power of all potions, charms, enchantments, witchcraft, bewitchments, sorceries and psychic entanglement on myself and on my family.

I also proclaim, accept, and decree that through the suffering of Jesus Christ and by His death on the cross and His resurrection from the dead that I have healing in my body, soul, mind and spirit. I AM HEALED, forgiven, set free and my sin debt has been paid in full! I AM JUSTIFIED, glorified, made righteous and set apart for the glory of God the Father!

And now, by the blood of Jesus Christ and the authority of the word of God I do now bind all of the powers of darkness, all demons, demonic forces, all ungodliness, all principalities, all lies, all false teachings, all hindering forces from demonic powers and/or from the acts of men and anything else that would hinder me in serving my Abba Father!

I cast them out as far as the east is from the west into the places that Jesus sent them to never to return to me or my family again. I lose the anointing of the Holy Spirit to break every demonic stronghold in my life and the lives of my family and to clean out the temple of my body, my mind and my soul so that I would be fit for my Heavenly Master's use.

And now, by the authority of the word of God, I call for restoration of everything that the enemy has taken from me and my family. I do reclaim and restore my birthright and inheritance as a child of the Most-High God. I call for the restoration of my peace, my joy and my health and my wellbeing. I call for the restoration of my family and my friends in my workplace, at home and in my finances. And by the word of God, I claim that in my life and in the lives of my family that the floors will be full of wheat and the vats will overflow with wine and oil! And the restoration of everything that the locust, the cankerworms, the caterpillars and the palmerworms have eaten up.

Finally, I do affirm and declare that in my life I will honor and glorify the name of the Most-High God, to whom be Glory, Honor and Praises forever! To my Lord and Savior Jesus Christ who is King of Kings, Lord of Lords and who is the redeemer of my soul. To the Holy Spirit, who is my teacher, my comforter and through his power the power of God flows into my life and the lives of my family. **TO GOD BE THE GLORY FOREVER, AMEN!!!**

James 4:7-11 Submit therefore to God. Resist the devil and he will flee from you. Draw near to God and he will draw near to you. Cleanse your hands, you sinners; and purify your hearts, you double-minded. Be miserable and mourn and weep; let your laughter be turned into mourning, and your joy to gloom. Humble yourselves in the presence of the Lord, and He will exalt you. Do not speak against one another, brethren. He who speaks against a brother, or judges his brother, speaks against the law, and judges the law, you are not a doer of the law, but a judge of it.

2 Timothy 3: 1-5 But realize this, that in the last days difficult times will come. For men will be lovers of self, lovers of money, boastful, arrogant, revilers, disobedient to parents, ungrateful, unholy, unloving, irreconcilable, malicious gossips, without self-control, brutal, haters of good, treacherous, reckless, conceited, lovers of pleasure rather than lovers of God; holding to a form of godliness, although they have denied its power; and avoid such men as these.

This is another prayer written by Win Worley for those in the bondage of sexual sin:

Lord Jesus, I have been involved in sexual sin, and I do now repent and confess to you that I have committed (here name specifically all of the sexual sins you can remember). I claim freedom for my body and mind from the bondage of sexual slavery and claim the promise that whosoever calls upon the Lord shall be delivered (Joel 2:32). Lord, you have promised that if I confess my sin, you will forgive my sin and cleanse me from all unrighteousness (1 John 1:9). I do now claim and accept your forgiveness and cleansing.

Satan, I rebuke you in the name of Jesus Christ my Savior, and I am notifying you now that in His name I am reclaiming every area of my mind and body which has formerly been given over to you and your hosts. Specifically, I claim freedom and cleansing in the areas of sexual sin and as a believer-priest I renounce you and your hosts and command that they leave me now in the name of Jesus Christ.

Chapter 7

People in the Bible who were deceived by the Spirits of Lust & Pride

F. Scott Fitzgerald said, "Show me a hero and I will write you a tragedy."

The spirit of Lust has caused a lot of problems in a lot of people in the Bible. Below are some of those people. Write down what you've discovered they lusted over.

1. Adam and Eve (Gen 3):

   _____

   _____

   _____

2. Samson (Judges 14 – 16):

   _____

   _____

   _____

3. King David (2 Sam 11):

   _____

   _____

   _____

4. Ahab & Jezebel (1 Kings 21):

_____

_____

_____

5. Sodom & Gomorrah (Gen 19):

_____

_____

_____

6. King Solomon (1 Kings 11: 1-6):

_____

_____

_____

The spirit of Pride has also caused a lot of problems in a lot of people in the Bible. Below are some of those people. Write down what you discovered they were prideful about.

1. Church of Laodicea (Revelation 3:14):

_____

_____

_____

2. Tower of Babel (Gen 11: 1-9):

_____

_____

_____

3. King Saul (1 Sam 15):

_____

_____

_____

4. Pharaoh (Exodus 7 – 12):

_____

_____

_____

5. Nebuchadnezzar (Dan. 4:37):

_____

_____

_____

6. Rich Man (St. Luke 12: 16-21):

_____

_____

_____

The Bible is the inspired word of God written down by man through the wisdom of the Holy Spirit. The Bible is our road map, our guide, our food and our salvation. The Word is Christ Jesus!

St. John 1: 1-5 *In the beginning was the Word, and the Word was with God, and the Word was God. ² He was in the beginning with God. ³ All things came into being through Him, and apart from Him nothing came into being that has come into being. ⁴ In Him was life, and the life was the Light of men. ⁵ The Light shines in the darkness, and the darkness did not comprehend it.*

Name one or more people in your life who has had a lustful addiction and this addiction affected your life as well.

_____

_____

_____

Have you forgiven this person?

St. Matthew 6: 14 & 15 *For if you forgive men for their transgressions, your heavenly Father will also forgive you. But if you do not forgive men, then your Father will not forgive your transgressions.*

There's freedom in forgiveness. What they may have done was terrible and scarred you deeply but, it wasn't them who did that to you. It was the evil spirits of lust that entered them and controlled them causing them to do what they did to you.

Unforgiveness is like someone yelling out curses to someone else while the whole time you're the one being cursed.

Unforgiveness is a spirit and it will not be satisfied until you take your last breath. It will take hold of you and bind you spiritually and mentally until the spirit of hate and rage own you.

When someone gets delivered from the spirit of unforgiveness they normally breath a deep breath and testify that they feel lighter, like a heavy weight has been lifted off of them. Many testify of not having anymore stomach problems and sleep all night instead of experiencing insomnia.

The road to recovery is not through drugs to suppress the pain but it's through deliverance in Jesus Christ.

Psalms 34: 4 I sought the LORD, and He answered me, And delivered me from all my fears.

Psalms 34: 17 – 19 The righteous cry and the LORD hears, and delivers them out of all their troubles. The LORD is near to the brokenhearted, and saves those who are crushed in spirit. Many are the afflictions of the righteous; but the LORD delivers him out of them all.

Conclusion

Don't be discouraged but be encouraged! Find a group of believers in Christ Jesus who believe all of God's Word and practice what He says we can do. Even churches under the title "Non-Denomination" can be seeker friendly, timed, and wouldn't touch deliverance with a 10 foot-pole. Find a church who doesn't seek out the approval of the people but seeks out the will of God. A church that will labor in the altar with a hurting soul and will go after the one crying desperately to be free.

Once we had a service go from 11am to 7pm because some people needed deliverance and healing. We ordered pizza at 4pm and rotated deliverance workers so they could eat. It was awesome! Once church Leaders stop worrying about keeping the '12:30 outta of here crowd' you'll start experiencing more freedom. Your numbers will drop off but that's called God grafting the tree so that it will produce more fruit! Can I hear an AMEN!!!

If God truly is in control at your church and you're allowing the Holy Spirit to run things, then you'll stop worrying about paying for that big ole building you got there. You'll watch Abba Father supernaturally supply the needs with less people. I know first-hand how that works, been there and got the T-Shirt!

There's hope! And His name is Jesus! Come and visit us, write us or email us and we'll be glad to share Jesus with you!

If you would like us to come and teach more about deliverance at your church please send us an email. Please send any prayer requests or testimonies of salvation and deliverance to:
Email: **pastortimandmissyjenkins@yahoo.com**

If you would like to visit us, our physical address is:
Freedom Crossing
497 Mountain Road
Clinton, TN 37716

Almost all of our Deliverance Team Members have regular jobs so time is limited to our services. We open up all of our services to Deliverance at Freedom Crossing.

<u>Services are as follows</u>:
Sunday School 10am
Sunday Worship & Preaching 11am
Sunday Night 5pm
Wednesday Night 6:30pm

<u>Freedom Crossing Church Social Media</u>:
Facebook, **www.freedomcrossingchurch.com** and You Tube. Learn even more about what God has in store for you and your family.

www.ingramcontent.com/pod-product-compliance
Lightning Source LLC
Chambersburg PA
CBHW060655030426
42337CB00017B/2632